Letters from Nana

Nana Barnett

A catalogue record for this book is available from the National Library of Australia

Copyright © 2021 Lynley Barnett

All rights reserved.

ISBN-13: 978-1-922727-03-9

Linellen Press
265 Boomerang Road
Oldbury, Western Australia
www.linellenpress.com.au

Dedication

This book is dedicated to Paige and Riley and was written for them during the pandemic when we couldn't be together.

Contents

Dedication 3
Contents 5
Letter one: June. 2020 7
Letter Two: June 11
Letter Three: June 14
Letter Four: June 16
Letter 5: June. 18
Letter 6: June. 21
Letter 7: June. 23
Letter 8: July 25
Letter 9: July 27
Letter 10: July 29
Letter 11: July 31
Letter 12: July. 32
Letter 13: July. 34
Letter 14: July. 36
Letter 15: July 38
Letter 16: July 39
Letter 17: August 41
Letter 18: August. 44
Letter 19: August. 46
Letter 20: August 48
Letter 21: August 50
Letter 22: August 52
Letter 23: September 54
Letter 24: September 57

Letter 25: September 59
Letter 26: October 61
Letter 27: October 62
Letter 28: November 63
Letter 29: November 64
Letter 30: December 66
Letter 31: December 67
Letter 32: December 68
Letter 33: December 69
Letter 34: December 71
Letter 35: January 2021 72
Letter 36 January 74
Letter 37: January 75
Letter 38: February 77
Letter 39: February 79
Letter 40: March 80

Letter one: June. 2020

I said today, "I am going to write a book."

And Poppy Graeme said, "What about?"

And I told him. He thought it was a good idea, and he loved the title of my book.

This is a book of letters.

These are letters to my grandchildren. Granddaughter, you are eleven as I write, and Grandson, you are nine.

So I start at the beginning, which is a very good place to start.

Hi Special People,

COVID has come into our lives, and because you live in Sydney, on the other side of Australia, and I live in Perth, now I cannot see you very often, so I am going to write to you.

I am going to tell you what happens over here in this huge state of Western Australia, and I am going to tell you that I miss seeing your smiles, and that I miss your cuddles. I am writing so you know that I am thinking of you a lot.

I told you, Granddaughter, that when you think of me you will have to remember just one thing: I love you to the Moon and Back.

Now you know when you look outside your window that, over the month, the moon becomes smaller and smaller until it is just a tiny crescent, then it starts to grow again until it is a full moon. When it is full, you can see all sorts of figures on the Moon, then you know how very far away it actually is.

I looked it up – it is 384,402 km away from us. Now to get there it would take a special airship powered by rockets, and it would take any time from 36 hours to a month, depending on the kind of airship you use. So when you think of that, you know that is how much you are loved.

I often wonder if you will ever go to the Moon, or Mars, because that may happen in your lifetime. Imagine, a trip in a spaceship going to the Moon. Well if you do get there, would you please plant a little Moon Flower for me.

And Grandson, how to tell you how much you are loved and cared about?

I can see your twinkly eyes as I tell you this, shall we say it is a much as the Soccer players can kick a ball around in a match of Soccer. Now that must be miles and miles in one game. You should know all about this because you play soccer.

I so remember taking you to the Glory Children's Soccer Day in WA when you met the players, and when they taught you soccer skills. How good you were at the game. I wonder if you will continue playing this sport, or if you decide to take up something else. We all have it in us to play a sport – we just have to find the one we like the most.

Letter Two: June

I think each of us has special skills. For some, it is the skill to play chess, and for others, it is the skill to run or to hit a tennis ball or to remember what we have read. The trick is to find your skills and then to enjoy them. Imagine what it would be like to be a famous Chef, and to be able to cook all sorts of food and set the food down on a table in front of people who just go "Aaaaah" with delight.

If I had that skill, the only problem would be that Poppy Graeme would never leave the kitchen. And you would hear his "Aaaaaah's" all over the house. What are your skills? Which ones do you know about today, and which ones will creep up and surprise you. What fun it will be when you discover you are really quite good at something you like to do.

My mother used to wish she could sing, but no matter how hard she tried, she just couldn't sing in tune. But by golly, she made the best breakfast ever. And words ... she knew so many words from her love of reading that she could astonish you with the words she used. And something else she could do that will make you chuckle ... she couldn't drive a car, but she could, and did, memorise all the bus routes she needed in the city of Auckland in New Zealand. She was better than a computer and could teach any new bus driver how to get almost anywhere in Auckland, which was no small feat. She had a wonderful sense of direction, and that is most unusual for a woman.

Auckland

Well she did not pass that sense of direction onto her daughters. I and my sister, Sandra, have absolutely no sense of direction. We can get lost anywhere. I think if you asked Sandra how many times she has been lost, and if I tried to add up all the times I have been lost, it would be hundreds.

During the day time, I look at the sun if I am really lost, but at night time I just stay lost. Since they invented the maps on our telephones and tablets, I have gone out and about and felt quite safe because I can always set the tablet to bring me home.

I once went into a Service Station in Sydney and cried all over the mechanic because I was so lost. He was the world's smartest man, as he showed me the route to the University. He told me which shops to look out for on the way, named about six, and hey presto I found the University entrance.

That is when I realised that we all have such different ways of learning. Some people are verbal, and some use their eyes and are visual. Do you know in what ways you learn best? It could be that you memorise well, or that you use a lot of memory joggers, like notes. Think about that! And that is the fun of learning, because you are learning about yourself along the way.

You know I like to read. I often think what a companion a book is. It is like having a friend with you. When I read, I get into the book and I know all the characters, and I think what they are thinking, and feel what they are feeling. I can be happy when they are happy and sad when they are sad. And sometimes the book is so exciting I just cannot put it down until I have finished it.

Why do I love reading? Well, when I was very young my mother introduced me to books. She took me to the Library, and she let me choose all sorts of books, lots and lots of them. Then every night I would climb into bed and read before my light was turned off. Later on when I was a grown up and went to University, I had to read all the books my teachers told me to. When I finished studying at the end of each year I would go back to the library and get an enormous pile of fun to read books. Then all summer long I would read into the night all the books that I enjoyed.

Now I am a Nana and no longer work, I still go to the Library and read to my heart's content - anything and everything. There is a word for people who read like me. This reading is called eclectic. So there you have a new word in your vocabulary. Eclectic.

Letter Three: June

I have been thinking: how would it be if I found a new word for you every so often? I'll write it down in my letter to you and by the time I have finished my book of letters you will have learned a whole new vocabulary. Now that will be a challenge for me and for you.

Mmmmm? What word can I come up with for this letter? Let me think.

OMNIBUS

We just say *the Bus*, but its real name is omnibus. That simply means a bus for everyone. The very first bus was pulled along by a horse in Paris, France in 1662. Poppy G and I get the bus into the city, or sometimes the train. That way we don't have to find a parking spot or pay the meter.

A trip to the city on a warm day is really great. We do some shopping, have lunch, and a catch-up with all the fashions in the shop windows. The people walking through the centre of the city all seem busy but happy.

Do you ever watch people's faces? I do. Some are really happy and smile a lot, and they walk with big strides to wherever they are going. Others look like they ate grumpy cornflakes for breakfast. So I dodge them. And I think to myself, I don't want their breakfast cereal – this is a day I want to enjoy.

We get a cup of tea and sit and people watch, and guess what they are doing today. I tried once at making up stories about people I saw in funny situations and what they might be up to. I did think that might be another book I could write. What do you reckon?

Letter Four: June.

I am going to have a Birthday this weekend, and Poppy G is giving me a surprise. He is taking me away for a few days. I am not allowed to know where I am going, except we will be taking the car, and our bicycles. So I am imagining all sorts of places. Will it be a hotel? Or a Motel? Never a tent! Much too cold! What about a Caravan Park and a Villa like we stayed in when you came to visit two Christmas's ago.

Didn't we have fun that time? I so loved having you, and watching you with other children, and making things, and swimming, and riding your bikes. Do you remember making the scarecrows? And the beautiful photo they took of you, my granddaughter, when you donated your scarecrow to the town. How many newspapers did we buy? About ten, just to get your picture at least ten times.

Did you see the Photo Book I made your dad to show him all the things you had done? Oh that was such a good time. I shall remember it forever.

And, dear Grandson, how I ran all around the Caravan Park looking for you when I thought I had lost you. And there you were all snug in a sleeping bag, watching a movie in another family's tent area. I thought I had said you could go out to play after tea, and you thought I had said you could go to the new family's tent area, and didn't we get our communication all messed up. But I do remember the huge hug we had when we realised that it was nobody's fault, just a huge mess up. You are a superb hugger, but I won't tell anyone because they might all want one.

Letter 5: June.

Today we had some wild weather, just for a short time. All part of winter-time. We need the rain to make the seeds grow and for all the plants to survive. I don't mind being out in the rain if I am all dressed up for it. The only bother I have is the rain on my glasses, because then I can't see where I am going.

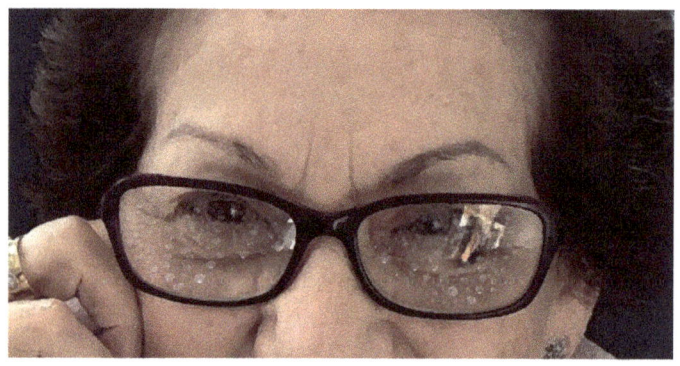

We watched the water trying to run down the drains but the drains couldn't keep up with the amount of water so water spread across the road. Then I saw a man drive his car into one huge mass of water and it rose up both sides of his car and almost swamped him.

I am going to let you into a secret. When you learn to drive, and you come to water spread across the road, you must slow down and go steadily through the water. Why is that, you ask? Because if you go full tilt into the water and it sprays all over you, you cannot see what is in front of you, and the water gets into your engine. And what happens next? You guessed it. Your engine stops.

I suspect you both will be good drivers later when you come

to learn to drive. And I wonder what cars you will drive? Will they be electric? Or fuel? Or will they be half fuel and half electric?

Hey, your next word is:

HYBRID

Hybrid. Hybrid means a bit of both. In this case, you have a tank of fuel and then all the batteries for electric driving. So the car is called a Hybrid car.

Do you remember the time we went on the Electric Bus in Perth, which was driverless? So clever! – it could miss people and things in the street. I still have my certificate to say I rode in the Driverless Bus. I think there will be a lot of those sorts of cars and buses when you grow up.

When I was a little girl, my dad had a very small car and you had to crank a handle at the front to make it go. It also had a roof you could take off to let in the fresh air and the sunshine. The only problem was that it could blow off in strong winds. I remember my brother cranking the car one day under a street light to start the car and, as he took a big breath, a large moth flew into his mouth. Because I was his sister I laughed and laughed, but he definitely did not think it was funny at all. But brothers and sisters do have a laugh at their siblings.

Is that another word for you?

It means your brother or your sister. And I'll bet, my granddaughter, you have had a laugh at your brother, and, my grandson, you have had a guffaw at your sister.

I have to write about the Coronavirus to you. Now it is called a pandemic. It is a disease that has spread across the world so quickly. Over thousands of years, there have been many diseases that have demolished large groups of people. But what makes this one different is that now we are so clever that we fly everywhere, or we cruise around countries and we take the disease with us. Way back when people travelled on horses, or even on trains, the disease could not go very far. Sailing ships did take diseases to other countries but there were not that many ships. We are so clever now because we can travel quickly almost all around the world, so we take disease with us everywhere.

I think this pandemic has taught us to be creative about our medicines, and what we need to help those who get sick. It has also taught us how we can help to stop the spread, so that if this should happen again, we will be so much wiser.

But the good that has come out of having to stay home during our shut down is something to wonder at. People have become more friendly, and neighbours so much nicer to one another. I think it is great that the kindnesses we have seen have warmed our hearts.

Letter 6: June.

Another day! Now I wonder what you two got up to today. It is a school day. Is your homework all done, school uniforms on, and your lunch in your bag? Another day, another adventure!

If you wake up each day and say to yourself what can I learn today, what can I get excited about today, who can I smile at today, or laugh with today, or kick a football with today, then your day is going to be great. You can start the day happy and have a brilliant day, or start the day grumpy and have a **'doleful'** day.

(That's your word for this letter.) Isn't it amazing that you can choose to have one or the other!

Any day I can start the day with a little sleep in, and breakfast with the newspaper, followed by some exercise, while I plan the other good things that I am going to make happen – that's a very, very good day. Poppy G starts every day with a smile, he is very good like that. He never wakes up grumpy. Can you believe that! He does have some crazy mad dreams though. He tells me when he wakes what he has dreamt of, then promptly forgets the dream.

What do you dream? Dreams are so special. They often have some messages in them for us. And usually, those messages are not hurtful but ideas we can learn from.

Sometimes they are just jumbled. Our brains are trying to sort our lives out and make sense of our world, and we seem to do this at night in our sleep. Just as well we don't do this during the day, otherwise we would be in a right mess.

If you want to remember your dreams, you need to write them down first thing in the morning because they seem to flit away quickly.

Letter 7: June.

It is still June and I have had a birthday. Poppy G took me up the coast to a beautiful fishing village called Jurien Bay. On the way up, Poppy G stopped at Cervantes, where we had lunch at the Crayfish Shack. Now that was to die for. The food was delicious and straight out of the ocean. Then on we went.

I thought of you two as soon as we arrived. It was a lovely place for children. Nice beaches, playgrounds, children everywhere. I just knew you would both have loved every bit of it. And, of course, you could fish to your heart's content. There was a little jetty for walks or fishing. The village itself had a lot of special fishing boats, and as they came in at the end of the day, they had large containers of freshly caught fish. Everyone there seems to make a living from fish. They freeze them and send them all over Australia, and overseas too. Who knows, the next time you eat Fish and Chips, you might be eating fish caught just off Jurien Bay.

I took away with me just my winter clothes and, would you believe it, the days were really warm and sunny. And this is winter time. But our seasons seem to have been changing, don't they. They seem to be getting later. Instead of summer being December, January and February, I think it starts in earnest in January and goes until the end of March, then it starts to cool down a little. So I believe all the seasons start about a month later than they did when I was a child. Perhaps the Aboriginal people have had the best idea all along. They think *there are 6 seasons and all of these are to do with what grows in Australia.*

Now what word can I think of for this letter? Mmmmm? I know:

Now that means stingy or mean. There was a really great book written by Charles Dickens about a very miserly man called Scrooge. He was so mean and so horrible until one Christmas when he realised that his meanness meant that he had no friends and no one loved him. Anyway, he changed his behaviour and became a good man. Charles Dickens books are called classic books. They were written a very long time ago, but they are still good to read even now. Charles Dickens wrote about the times he lived in, the town he knew, and the people he met in his life, so we end up knowing a lot of the history of England through his writings.

Letter 8: July.

It has skipped into July, and now the nights are cold. But we are still happy, cold or warm, and there is still such a lot to do and such a lot of life to live.

We have bought another caravan. So the next few weeks we will be getting the electrics on the car to match up to the van, and kitting out the van.

I have all my cups and plates and cutlery, but everything needs a wash before it goes into the caravan. So I am beginning to feel like a washer-woman. Did you know way back when people did not have washing machines, some women would take everyone's washing and do it, all day long. Then get it dried and return it to the owner. Can you imagine their hands? They would be all wrinkled up from water and soap. I don't think I would have liked that.

I was having a little conversation in my head with you two a few days ago, and it went like this:

I wonder if you wonder why you are here on this earth. It is the biggest question in the world to think about. So here is what I think – we are on this earth to do the best we can to and for as many others as we can.

So that means that every day we try to use all our skills for the good of our community. **Community,** *that's your word for this letter. Community means all those that live near and around us. All these people we try to share a little of our lives with. We try to make their days a tiny bit happier. Now, if you think hard about this, you will realise that if we were all doing that, the world would be without wars and a much happier place. So it's sad that everyone doesn't realise that they are actually here on this earth for a purpose, and that purpose is definitely not to be mean to anyone.*

Letter 9: July.

How come some people in this world are mean and nasty? That's my big question for this week. What would you answer to that? Would you say: Because they got out of the wrong side of the bed that day? No. I think they learned to be that way. They learned that they got their own way by being mean and cruel. Or they did it because when they were younger, someone else did it to them so now they use payback - except that they pay back everyone.

So what can you do when someone is just cruel and nasty to you?

Well, the very best and smartest way to behave is to walk away from them. Don't let them hurt you. Find another friend who you know you like, and who likes you in return. Their company is much better to have.

I believe that the greatest present you can give yourself is a friend. And to have a friend, you first need to be a friend. To like someone who is a little like yourself, someone who talks and acts really well with you. Someone who cares about you! Someone who will "have your back" in the bad times! This person knows you and loves you even when you make mistakes, say the wrong thing, or do something incredibly stupid. They like you in spite of that. But remember what I said, to have a friend, you need to be a friend. So you have to show this person that you accept them just as they are, even when they act rubbish-like, you still know that deep down they are nice people. And they can be boys or girls - it really doesn't matter. Friends are not made by their gender. One of your Aunties had a friend when she was about 6 years old, and he was about 90 years old. She always stopped by his garden on the way to school, and they would talk about all sorts of things. He was a beautiful, kind and gentle man, who loved his talks with her. So age and gender don't have to matter, but you do need a collection of friends around your own age who you can spend time with before and after school - ones you can just have some fun with.

You do know, don't you, that love is something that is like a bottomless pit. There is so much of it in you that you can keep on giving it - it will never run out. So don't be mean with your love. Make friends and share your kindnesses with them because I will let you into a secret. The more love you have to share, the more will come back to you. And if you ever find someone who doesn't want your kindnesses, just let them be. There will be a lot more out there who will appreciate everything about you. And secretly isn't that exciting to think about. Wow ten times over.

Letter 10: July

The great thing about a Nana, and a Poppy, is that you can say almost anything to them, and they will keep it all a secret if you ask them to. Mind you, if you are being physically hurt, that might not be secret material. But they are people who are old enough and smart enough to see that their very special grandchildren have lots of ideas and thoughts that should be encouraged. And, they want to know all about you and how you are getting on. They really do want to know because they are interested in you. So when you think about that you realise they are not just grandparents, but special friends too.

Isn't that a really nice thought?

"Special friends", the kind that you can turn to at any old time at all, and you can even rant and rave a bit at too. When the whole world seems determined to make you unhappy, you can just say it as it is 'blah blah and blah', and they will understand. A long time ago, I read a definition of a friend which said 'it is that person who sees the wheat, and the chaff and the weeds', and with kindness blows the weeds and chaff away.

I wonder, if I gave you the word **Kindness** *for this letter, how you would describe it. Being nice to or doing something nice for another? So let's think about that.*

I am going to describe it like this: kind is like me, my kind.

So when I do something for another, I think it is what I would like another to do for me. And then I think, I can't be too wrong if what I want for them is what I would like for myself. Sometimes all I might want is a smile, and if I give that smile to another and get one in return, it has just made my day. This is such a big subject we could talk about it all day, but for today your word to think about is:

"Kindness".

Letter 11: July

Today your letter begins in a hairdresser's shop because Nana is waiting for a haircut, and everyone is busy.

Isn't it interesting learning how to wait? You wait for Birthdays and Christmas, and the bus, and maybe a taxi. But we have waiting time just about every day, don't we.

So let's have some fun while we wait. Don't get grumpy, that just spoils your day. Instead, how clever can you be while you wait? You could count the people who go by the shop front - there are so many things in a Shopping Centre you could count. What could you name?

You see, your bright, clever brains can be asked to do things to keep you occupied. You just have to press the "on" button. The minute you do that, all the cogs in your brain start moving, and soon you will come up with an idea that's fun and sometimes even a bit crazy. And who cares. Just keep yourself involved and happy, sometimes busy, and that dreaded word "bored" will never be one that you use. That word is one that I never knew existed until I was an adult and heard others using it.

"Bored?" Never! I couldn't waste one minute of my life being "bored". And seriously, isn't it a waste of time. No, there are things to do and places to be and sights to see, and I want to do them all. I still want to do them all, and I suspect that you do too.

Letter 12: July.

I went to church this past weekend. And because of COVID 19 we all have to sit with one whole pew empty in front of us and one empty behind us. That's to keep Social Distancing. So everyone is careful to do as we are asked.

While I was in church, I had a little talk to my mother, who I believe is up there in heaven. When we die and our body is no longer any use to us, I think that our soul, that part of us that makes us "Us", goes on its merry way up to God. So I believe that your great-Nana is up in heaven because she was such a good person while she lived on earth. While I am having a chat to her, I ask her to look down over you two, and keep you safe. Now I know she is not the Boss 'Up there'. but I hope she can talk to God and just let him know that you are very special grandchildren and would He mind just making sure you are ok.

People call having a chat to God prayer. Well, I don't think it matters much what you call it. But being able to have a chat to God is kind of nice. Well, I think so. I have always felt quite certain that there is a "Someone" who created all of us, our world, and our universe, and most of us just call that person God because we need a name for Him.

This is how I have reasoned it: I believe that nothing cannot create something. So, there has to be a beginning of the world as we know it. And no matter how far back you go, something *began the creation. And if it cannot be nothing, then there is a God.*

It's a mystery, isn't it? Some scientists will say that we were created after the "Big Bang", and that may be true that planets and moons were created that way, but what created the ingredients that made up the "Big Bang. Mmmmm. Think about that.

It's a good topic to discuss because lots of ideas are out there about how we all came into being. Your great-Nana died twice, and the first time she came back after being away from us physically. She told us she had been sitting 'At the hem of His gown' and did not want to come back to earth. The second time she did not come back to us, so I always have this picture in my head of her happily snuggled up at the Hem of His Gown. And that makes me feel so happy that she has a special place and is being looked after.

Letter 13: July.

There might be questions that you think about and some that you cannot find answers to. That happens to all of us. Funny questions, like why do we need toes? Or why can't we all have blue eyes or brown skin? We wouldn't get sunburnt then, would we? Or they might be serious questions like: Why am I a girl, or why am I a boy?

These are great questions to ask Dads and Mums, and teachers, because most of those questions have real explanations. And when you ask the BIG questions, you can have a wonderful talk with others about what you have been puzzling over. That is one of the ways to make your education work for you. Never be afraid to ask questions because the answers may be really fascinating to get. And one day, when you have children of your own, you may be able to share what you learnt when you were growing up.

The funniest question I ever asked was 'what is a swear word'? I had no idea because my Dad and my brothers didn't swear. I knew that there were words I was not supposed to use, because back then they called them 'bad" words'. Except that I didn't even know what they were. So I asked, and I was told, and then I thought 'OK, I don't have to use them,' but at least now if someone swears at me, I will know he or she is pretty angry. Now I have a big laugh at what I didn't know. And as you know I love words.

I am thinking about a word for this letter. I know: **hemisphere!** What is it?

It's a half of a sphere and you have two spheres where?

Why, in your brain, of course.

Your brain is divided into two hemispheres. You have the left hemisphere, which weirdly enough controls the right side of your body, and the right hemisphere, which also weirdly enough controls the left side of your body.

We know the right side of the brain controls how we see things, even how we 'see' space, and it is where our emotions come from.

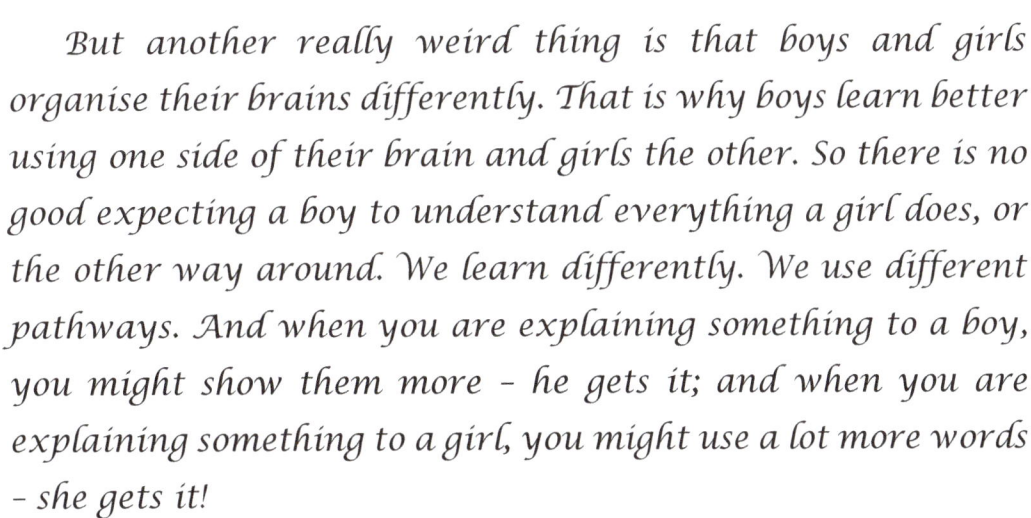

The left side of the brain is the side that controls language and practical and concrete thinking.

So we really need both sides of our brains to make us function properly.

But another really weird thing is that boys and girls organise their brains differently. That is why boys learn better using one side of their brain and girls the other. So there is no good expecting a boy to understand everything a girl does, or the other way around. We learn differently. We use different pathways. And when you are explaining something to a boy, you might show them more - he gets it; and when you are explaining something to a girl, you might use a lot more words - she gets it!

Letter 14: July.

Do you ever have a wish? Like I wish that I could fly on a magic carpet anywhere in the world. Well, I used to wish that I could fly like a bird, just soar off into the sky, and then look down towards earth. I think it would be so quiet up there, no noises from traffic, or buildings being made. And imagine how far you could see? You could see all around you, and miles and miles in front of you. I reckon that's why some people become Pilots because the sky is so interesting and inviting.

Now I never want to go down to the bottom of the sea - that would be too scary for me. And I never ever want to go climbing through caves like some people do. That would spook me forever. But up there in the sky, with blue everywhere, that would be so exciting, so peaceful.

What sort of wishes do you have? Are they wishes you could actually make come true, or perhaps a wish because you would like to undo something that happened? If it is a wish to undo something and it can't be undone, you have to find a way that lets you just accept the change. That's tricky, but it can be done. I think you just find what is good about the way your world is now, even without being able to undo some change or other, and you learn to love that special good thing.

Let's make up a scenario and see if my thinking could work. Say you wanted to undo the fact that you can't sing for toffee apples. You really have a terrible singing voice, darn it. Well, what is good about that? Mmmm! It's good that you like music, and that you can really listen to it and let it warm your body and soul. Maybe you can't sing along with it; maybe you can just hum. But you can appreciate it, and you can listen to it and let it take you away into that special world of music where the singing makes everything feel good in this world. Just imagine that, clouds of song. Now I don't know if you can make clouds of song but my imagination can make those clouds. Can yours?

That's your word for this letter:

Imagination.

Imagination is exciting. It lets you know characters in books. It lets you draw scenes from a book. It lets you pretend you are a prince or a princess. It lets you live for a little while on a beautiful desert island with nothing but sunshine, and beautiful beaches and plates of ice cream.

If you could imagine a beautiful scene with you as the centre piece, what would the scene be? Think about this very carefully because: this is the scene I want you to remember, so that any time you feel glum you can take yourself into that place and just feel content. No one has to know where it is … it can just be your secret. One day if you whisper it into my ear, I will tell you my secret place.

Letter 15: July

I have a word for this letter – it is: *random*. You can have a random thought. You can play a card game where the cards are dealt randomly. It means something that happens without conscious thought or decision. It just happens. An example of a random thought might be as you are skipping along the footpath and you think: I wonder what's for tea. The question just popped into your head.

So what use is random? Now that's a good question. I am asking myself the question and thinking, well, if it is random, it means no one made it happen. If a pink and grey parrot landed in front of me in the garden, that would be random – it would also be quite exciting.

I wonder how much of what happens to us is just random. Lots of people think nothing is random, that all actions and happenings are part of a bigger plan. But I'm not convinced that others have a plan for me. I think that I may have a plan for me, but it's a pretty mixed-up plan. I wonder what you think. Do you plan a lot, or does a lot of your day just happen?

Letter 16: July

Today as I came out of my swimming exercise class, I looked up and the sky was weird. The sun was shining and warm, the sky was blue and pretty, and right in the middle was a long black cloud. It was absolutely full of rain. So I drove home with the sun in the window of the car, and the black cloud looking ferocious. Miraculously, it didn't rain. It went over the top of me, and I knew by the time it reached the hills it would drop great bucket loads of rain. It made me think.

Do you know how it happens when you wake up and get up and some parts of you are happy, and some parts of you are not? That's just like the sky with the black cloud right smack dab in the middle of it. So what do you do? Well, you sure don't wait for the rain to drop on top of you; you look at how you might enjoy the sun. I think it is easy to get miserable when things go wrong. And it is hard to find the sunny places. But that's the trick of keeping yourself happy. You look for the nice person to talk to, you look for the company of people who are positive about life, you try to put lots of those people in your life, and you put a smile on your dial, and watch how it takes over and makes happy thoughts come along.

And there is a little secret I will share with you. If you have a dog, or a cat, or an animal you love, find them and have a special moment with them, because they love you no matter what. When your uncle was a little boy, he would find the dog and the two of them would go into the dog's kennel and I would

 hear him telling the dog all his worries and woes. And what did the dog do? She made him feel better because she just listened and cosied up to him. She could be his best friend and his comfort. She knew just what to do.

So today's letter is all about the word:

DEPRESSION

Happiness is the exact opposite of depression. We all get "it" (depression) from time to time, but we are also blessed with the ability to get away from the black cloud and into the sunshine again. Think about that. We really are clever people you know. And have a special something that helps you when you get a bit depressed. What could it be? Have you tried a cuddle with your favourite soft toy perhaps, or a cuddle with the dog? Perhaps it is a book that just makes you forget? Or can you write something down?

Here is a special way of making depression move away. Take your pen and paper. Write down your sad thoughts in any old scribbly way. Then take them outside to the large rubbish tin and tear the paper up into little pieces, and drop them in the bin. Next, go and curl up with your favourite book, get warm and snug and let the story take you away on a magic carpet. It works every time. Or when you get older, you could ring Nana up and she will be your extra special anti-depressant.

Letter 17: August

I'm thinking, I'm thinking. What could be the word for today? I know,

Marzipan

What's that, you say? Well, it is icing that goes onto very special cakes. It could be a Wedding cake, a Christmas cake, or a Birthday Cake. It is an icing that you only make for special occasions, and it is very rich to taste. It is an icing that will twist and turn, and one that you can make figures with, or create pictures with, just by shaping it and adding special colours to it.

Don't you just love the way thoughts pop into your head! You see, thinking about special occasions made me think of

cake, and special cakes made me think of Marzipan. And guess what Marzipan made me think of? Yes, My mother. She used to make Christmas Cakes and put a Marzipan Icing on them. She always tried to make Christmas so special for us all. Back in the days when I was very young, we didn't have a lot of money so my mother grew our vegetables, and baked our cakes, and always at Christmas time, she would spend ages making the most delicious cakes. Now when I see a decorated cake I think of how she made Christmas into a lovely occasion for us all. Roast Chicken with all the trimmings, and hot puddings and lots of fun. There was always a super-sized bone for the dog, and he would spend all day chewing on it. I don't remember what she gave the cat, but I suspect she gave her the left-overs from the chicken. We shared the day with the animals – they were never left out.

And Christmas time is a time of giving, isn't it. We give presents, sometimes just little things, but they are given with love. And we remember those people who do not have as much as we do, and we give a donation of money to help them have a better Christmas.

One day, when Poppy G and I were travelling overseas in a country near Russia, we saw a little girl; she was about 6 years old. And she put out her hand to us. She was begging because she did not have many of the good things that you and I have. I wanted to give her all the money I had in my purse. But then I had a second thought. I wondered if she'd had breakfast. So my friend and I bought her a breakfast, and she smiled the biggest smile. We gave her some coins to take home to her family as well. In so many countries in the world, people do not have enough to eat, or clothes to keep them warm. So when you see someone you can help, even with the smallest gift, you give them that little help, and I can tell you this, you will feel a lovely feeling knowing that someone ate today because of you.

I wish all the children in the world were well-fed, but I know that cannot happen until all the World Leaders stop wars and share generously what they have. So, until then, we all have to pray that little children, like the girl we met, get a meal from a stranger.

Letter 18: August.

What do you know about **Bullying?** Now there's a word for today. It is so strange because originally bully meant a really excellent person. But that all changed over the years and now, of course, it means someone who seeks to hurt or harm another. When they hurt, or harm another they feel like a "big" person. But they are not big in my eyes, and I don't think they are "big" in your eyes either. Those cruel people only do it to others who they think won't fight back, or can't fight back – so what does that make them? I think it makes them just "big" cowards. I think if you feel bullied you have to get reinforcements to help you. Those reinforcements could be teachers or mum or dad.

And this is the reason for getting help. One: because you cannot always manage bullies on your own. And two: the bully needs to be shown how to change their behaviour. We want them to learn new behaviours so that others do not get hurt by them. A bully never stops at bullying one person, they just go on and on, and to stop that they require a lot of help in their lives.

So, if you see bullying, it's not ok. It is never ok. And adults are needed to sort the bully out.

Poppy G tells the story of a chap on a plane who decided to pick a verbal fight with another young man, a friend of his. The bully was loud and nasty and cruel. And the young man *did nothing, but kept the peace. Eventually, the bully left him alone and went back to his seat. And we laugh about it now. Why? Because the bully didn't recognise the young man, he was so rude to. He was a boxer who had many titles to his name and who could have knocked the bully into outer space if he had wanted to. But he didn't. Why? Because he knew his hands were like lethal weapons. And also, because he is actually a peace-loving person, he made a choice. He did not let the bully's words upset him. Now that's what I call smart! But, honestly, can you imagine trying to pick a fight with a world boxing champion?*

Sometimes you might even be aware that you have been a bit demanding yourself. Maybe you weren't bullying, but you were really nasty to a friend. Well, that is not the end of the world. What it needs is for you to be smart enough to go back to the friend, and apologise. 'I'm sorry,' is not always easy to say, but it can repair a friendship.

Letter 19: August.

Now, let talk about **"I'm sorry."**

These are two words that we find very hard to say. Especially when you know that what you have done was really pretty awful. You were angry, or upset, or just in a very bad mood. And you took your entire bad mood out on another person. Oooooops.

You know they didn't deserve it. It really was you, your fault, and your bad mood. Not theirs. That's the time when you "man" up, or "woman" up. And as soon as you can, you go and make an apology to them. Now for an apology to really be sincere it has to go like this:

"I am sorry for what I said, please forgive me."

Not "I am sorry for what I said but you really made me get mad." Why? Because that's an unbelievable apology. That's blaming them for your bad mood.

Be sincere, just be simple when you apologise. And hope they will accept it and forgive you. And if they don't, well you may have to let some time go by before they feel ok with you. Remember, you caused it, not them.

But here's a truth: apologies sincerely given are the very best way of accepting that you helped to cause the problem, and others respect you for your ability to be able to say those magic words.

So in your special box, tucked away inside your thinking, "I'm sorry" rates along with:

"Thanks for your help."

"Thanks for thinking of me."

"What can I do to help?"

And the most magic one of all. "I love you".

Now those words you reserve for the special people in your life.

While I am on about these words, there is something else I should bring up. There are lots of times in our lives when something is done for us which is helpful, and which we appreciate. And how absolutely marvellous it is when we say what we have appreciated. That means that you might come up with all sorts of words, or phrases to show appreciation.

"Great tea. Thanks, Mum, or Dad."

"Thanks for the help with my maths, Mrs Jones."

"Fred, you showing me how to kick the soccer ball was fantastic."

"Granddaughter: thanks for collecting my clothes for me."

"Grandson: would you like to play a game of xxxxx with me?"

Lots of ways that you can show you are grateful for extra help, friendship, or kindness. So, put them in your grab a bag of good ideas, and be ready to use them often.

Letter 20: August

Your Nana likes to write. You know that, don't you. She loves words, she loves reading, and she loves writing. Well, some of us like to show our feelings in other ways. Some actually "do" things that show love. They are not word people. And that's ok.

Some people do things from a distance, quietly. And that's ok.

Some people talk their feelings and thoughts, and that's marvellous. We would describe these people as orators, those who can turn words into pictures for us. And then there are those people who capture feelings in art work, pictures, paintings and photos. They can express themselves in great works that live for centuries. So, we all have a way to express ourselves.

And what use is it to know this?

Well, often you may want to have a friend say something and they can't, but they can write it, or draw it. We have to look at our friends with a big open heart, and allow them to "talk" in the way that suits them. I know a very loving man who builds. He makes steps, and cupboards, and shelves, and beds, and so many things that I could never do. And he does all this for the person he loves dearly. So this is his way of talking and showing his feelings. When you think about that, doesn't it make his building skills so precious? All done to show love!

You could stop and think now, how do you show love, affection, thanks, or even crossness? That is you. And your skills are your skills. What it teaches you is to look for those "other" skills in people, because you might miss something very special if you just expect them to be like you.

Now, I have to think of a word for today's letter.

Oh, I have a huge beautiful word - *Onomatopoeia*. Can you say it? Try. This is a fun word and what it means is this. This is when the word you use imitates a sound. It could be a word like Clackety Clack. Or perhaps it could be a word like snap, or hiss. Those words give you an image in your mind. Like, if I said Buster the bird HISSED at me, you know straight away what the sound is, *and* that he is really grumpy when he does that. Hisssssss. It is a great word.

Well, that is using Onomatopoeia.

Now you may forget this huge word, but you will remember that some words create an image and knowledge of a sound. And you will remember that your Nana told you about this. I think that this sort of thing happens a lot. We remember odd things because someone told us about it. That person conjures up the strangest memories. Can you think of a person or an animal that creates an odd memory for you?

Letter 21: August

Do you know what **Poetry** *is?*

It is a way of communicating, using words, rhymes, and rhythms that are crafted in such a way that they paint a picture. Poetry selects words carefully, sometimes not a lot of words, and then creates an image with those words.

Every culture in the world has done this, so there are lots of forms of Poetry. And some poet's works are considered very precious because they tell us of the times in which they lived.

You know the Winnie the Pooh Books? Well, the little boy who owned Winnie the Pooh was Christopher Robin and there is a lovely poem about him. It starts:

"Little Boy kneels at the foot of his bed

Droops on his little hands, little gold head

Sssshhhhhh whisper who dares

Christopher Robin is saying his prayers"

Look on the internet for the rest of the poem. It is beautiful. Poetry is a form of writing that both men and women have done for hundreds of years. And you can write your own, and have some fun with words that rhyme.

Let me see if I can make a little poem about you two:

"My grandchildren

Should dance on a stage

Because He can do skips

And she can do flips

If they do it together

In fine sunny weather

They'll both make you laugh

By being so daft."

Now how about that for a crazy poem! Have a go one day when you have a rainy day and you are thinking of what to do! You might try writing about Nana and Poppy.

Your word for this letter is **inspiration**.

Inspiration is when you have a sudden brilliant idea to do something. It might be to cook something special. It might be to do cartwheels in the park. You can share your inspirational ideas, like I am sharing mine. When I said to Poppy G that I was going to write a book, that was an inspirational idea. Now all these pages later, here is the essence of the book: Thoughts I am sharing with my grandchildren.

Letter 22: August

Your word for today is *blustery*.

Why? I chose that word because outside my door the weather is blustery. It is windy, and cold, and the rain is whirling around, not falling straight down. It hits the windows, then the doors, then the plants. It is sort of all over the place.

Well, people can be blustery too. Usually when they are uncomfortable, or they get caught out doing something they didn't want you to know about, and they start saying things that are 'all over the place'. You might recognise it in other people, but it is also helpful when you recognise it in yourself. When you find yourself talking rubbish and being 'blustery' it is usually a good time to stop and listen to the other person. You might then hear something that you can do to make them feel better about you. Just a thought!

Do you ever make plans? That is when you put together your thoughts and get them organised. Say you want to go to the pictures with your friend. You create a plan. You might ask your parents if you can go, and your friend if they can go. You might find out if the bus runs past the theatre. You might check your money box to see if you can afford to go. Now that would be very important. So at the end of making plans, you would find a way to go to the pictures with your friend. Plans help us to get what we would like to achieve. And then there are the times when you make no plans and just go with the flow, and see what happens.

That's fine too, that is called being **spontaneous** (another word!) There are people who always make plans, or who always act spontaneously. Well, that isn't so smart either. Just imagine if you never did anything without a plan. Heavens you might never go anywhere on a lovely sunny day. Or just imagine if you act spontaneously all the time you would never get tickets to your favourite singers or band, because you have to book these things a long way in advance, don't you. So, there are times when planning is very important, and then there are times when just doing it when it happens because you feel like it is right. It needs a balance, I think.

I'm lucky. I am a planner by nature, and Poppy G is a spontaneous person, so in the mix of things we both create happy days for each other. This is the way we can both make good things happen. When you don't have a Poppy G, you have to be careful to get a balance, and not to growl when others want you just to 'join in'. The secret is this … "don't miss out on having fun in your life. Try both planning and being spontaneous."

Goodness me, you have had two words this letter. How did that happen?

Letter 23: September

What is a birthday?

It is the one day of the year that is yours. That's the day when everyone in your family remembers you, and often gives you a present, if you are lucky. Sometimes you cannot celebrate your birthday until the weekend, but that's ok too, it is still YOUR day.

I think a Birthday should be a day of smiles. It's a day when you have a lot of fun with family, and with friends. If you could wish for something special for your Birthday, what would it be? Would you wish for a trip to the Circus? Or would you wish for a visit to the Zoo? Maybe a visit to Adventure land with friends? I have been thinking hard about what would make a Birthday extra special.

The first thing I would want would be a very sunny day and a fantastic breakfast somewhere special. Can you imagine that? Well, I can tell you about a Birthday that I had in two different countries. On the same day! We were travelling with *a group. At the start of my birthday, we were in Greece then we went to the Island of Capri in Italy. It was indeed the most wonderful Birthday. Breakfast in Greece and Dinner in Italy, and because it was so wonderful, I will always remember it.*

Which of your birthdays do you remember?

I am looking for a word for this letter. And I have found one. **Regret.** *What does that mean? Well, I think it means that something you have done has caused a problem perhaps for yourself, or maybe for someone else. And you tell yourself afterwards that you wish you had not done that. It is ok to have regrets because you can always learn from them.*

What I know is this: we all make mistakes. And we all can learn to do better. And that is what makes us human – learning. Out of all the things that we learn the most important thing is to find a way to love and appreciate.

So here is an idea.

You could start a little book, and write in it every day, or every other day, "I am grateful for" and then write something that you are REALLY grateful for.

Think of what you might write. I am grateful for my friend, Susie. I am grateful for my nice warm bed. I am grateful for our dog, Charlie. And as you write these things down you find that you really do appreciate having them in your life. You might even write "I am grateful for my teacher, who showed me how to do my maths assignment." Or "I am grateful for my sister/brother because I know they love me with all my faults."

Uggggggh! I can just hear you say - I am never going to write THAT down.

Well, I hope you might write ... I am grateful for my Nana and Poppy G because I know that even though we are miles apart, they love us to the Moon and Back.

And that's a lot of love.

Letter 24: September

Do you ever just sit and wonder? Like you just watch the clouds crossing the sky and wonder why they are going so slowly? Or where did they come from? That is your word for this letter.

Wonder

Wonder? If you sit and wonder, you are thinking about what or why, and thinking about why things happen, or maybe why they don't happen. And that leads you to be curious, and being curious is a good thing. It is just a way of learning. Usually when you are curious you want to find an answer. Provided you look for your answer in a safe way, it will teach you heaps.

But you could wonder why, and it might not be safe to look for the answer by yourself. Let me give you an example. Poppy G and I were fast asleep one night when something woke me up. It was a noise that I couldn't understand. So I woke Poppy G up, and asked him to come with me to find out what the noise was. We got up and crept quietly out of the house, listening to people talking and calling out. They were out on the street, and their noise had woken me up. Poppy G can sleep through anything, he didn't wake up! It really wasn't anything except some young people who were coming home late, singing, and laughing, talking and having some noisy fun. So we toddled back to bed. But together we went out because two persons are better than one. So, remember that, sometimes when you wonder, it helps to share the wonder and the curiosity because who knows what the answer might be.

Being safe is very important. That simply means that you look after yourself, and that if you don't feel comfortable with someone you don't stay with them, play with them, walk or go anywhere with them. You'll know if you feel uncomfortable, and you know to speak to an adult if you have had an uncomfortable moment. What you don't know is that almost every one of us has had an uncomfortable moment, so we all know exactly what you are talking about. It is so ok to tell an adult.

Letter 25: September

What do you do when you have a very big disappointment? Do you cry? Well, that's ok. I have cried too when something didn't happen that I was so looking forward to. I know it is ok to cry, and Poppy G knows it is ok to cry. It is so lovely to get a really big hug when a disappointment happens. You wait and wait for something nice that is going to happen, and poof it disappears. I have sometimes said, I'll be ok after I have a good cry, then I will feel better. And I do. Tears are just our expression of a sad time in our lives, but here's the thing. Smiles are an expression of glad times in our lives, and they're ok too.

We are made up of lots of emotions. Oooh, here we go - another word. The word is:

EMOTIONS

Basically, they all boil down to ... the sad, glad, and mad emotions. Every one of those emotions has a place. They have a time when they are just right. Stub your toe and what do you feel? Hurt and mad, and you jump around grabbing your foot and you want to smack the leg of the chair, (not the most sensible idea, of course.) But well you are good and mad, aren't you? And I think you are allowed to have all those emotions, for a little while. But when my toe feels better, I get on with what I was doing. I would love to stay really happy and excited, but imagine if I was like that all day. I think I would be exhausted at the end of it. So we have lots of emotions, and we can enjoy the happy ones, and find ways to calm the sad ones.

That is just a part of being me.

So what good is it in knowing this? Well, I think that, if I can be like that, then others will be like that too. So sometimes my friends want to laugh with me and sometimes they might want to cry with me, and here's the secret.

It's ok. They are just being themselves.

Letter 26: October

It's puzzle time. What word can I think of today? I know,

 *'Peace'.*

Peace is that lovely feeling when you wake up in the morning and it is fine and sunny, the dog is waiting for you with hugs and love, your breakfast is warm and tasty, and absolutely no one is grumpy. You feel at peace. Well, sometimes you have to create peace for yourself because there is no one else around to do it for you. So how do you create peace?

Ooooh, isn't that a good question. Nana has to think hard.

First, I think you have to tune your brain into peace. You have to think: Today is going to be a good day. Today I am going to be happy. Then as the day unfolds you have to look at everything positively, and when your day is coming to an end you can sit somewhere and relax and breathe in the Peace. I think peace is being tranquil. When your mind and body is just being, not rushing anywhere but when you let your mind and body go quiet and you allow everything to wash over you in the nicest possible way. I can feel the peace as I type this. And it feels great! Peace: isn't it a beautiful word, even when you say it, it feels sort of velvety and smooth.

Letter 27: October

I have a very special word for today. It is *HOPE*.

You want something, or you want something to happen, so you hope it will happen.

Sometimes your hopes can be huge ones, and other times your hope may be just a tiny hope. Well, never let go of the hope, because that comes from deep inside of us. And when we hope, we hope for very special things. Usually they are so special, so important for us. We often don't tell anyone about our hopes - perhaps the hopes might be laughed at - perhaps they are just so very private that we cannot share them? And all of that is OK. Except of course when your Nana is around, because she is the very person you can share your hopes with. I think you would find that she has hopes that she can share with you too. So one day when no one is looking we can have a 'Treasure Chest of Hopes party'.

Yay, we can share all the hopes we have, and I won't tell if you promise not to tell either. Is it a deal?

Letter 28: November

Today I feel like giving you some mad, mad words. So here goes. What is a ==quadrupedal ruminant mammal?== Give in?

Answer: A sheep. Those words describe a four-legged mammal who chews its food more than once. Now who would have thought that someone chose to name a poor animal in that way because it had four legs and chewed its food the way it does.

Good grief! What names would they come up with for us? Well, I know a couple – one is Homo sapiens. This comes from the Latin language and means 'wise man'. And, of course, we get called humans too.

If you studied Latin you would know that a lot of words we use come originally from Latin. And Latin comes from Roman times. So it is a very old language.

I am hoping that each of you learns another language. How great it must be to be able to speak to people from other countries in their own language. If you lived in Europe, you would be very likely to learn several languages. How lucky are the children who learn to speak all the European languages, French, Spanish, Italian and many more.

Letter 29: November

It's time to find a word. I have one: **illusion**.

Magicians use Illusions, which is really a false idea or belief. It's a bit like a trick. Magicians use it for fun and wonder.

And we can use illusions too. We can create illusions, like ghosts. We can dress up as something else to make an illusion. So you just pretend. And that's ok too, just so long as you don't stay pretending all the time.

When you feel up to it you can then take down the illusion and speak the truth. The only idea I have about this is that you don't leave it too long before you explain the truth.

And that makes me think about truth even more. It seems like a weighty word, and I think it is. Truth can be helpful and not helpful. Sometimes waiting until the other person is ready before we tell them the truth helps them to hear what it is you want to say.

But - and this is a big but - it is not always our place to speak the truth to another. Sometimes it just isn't our business. Let's say you see Penelope cheating in an exam. What should you do? Isn't that a tough question?

Well, I would speak to her, and tell her she needs to own up to it, but is it my business to tell on her? You are going to get mixed answers to that question. So I am going to say this is how I would decide. How important is it in telling the truth in this case? And if the answer is not important then I will mind my own business. If the answer is very important, then I would look at who might need to know this truth.

I think if you asked 100 people this question, 50 would say tell, and 50 would say don't tell. So, it is a really vexed question that I posed, and one that might have more than one answer. So, you might need to take some advice from an adult about whether to speak or not.

Do you like the word *vexed*. A problem or difficult issue, or one that makes you really annoyed. The word rolls off your tongue. Can you make a sentence with the word vexed in it? Try.

Letter 30: December

We are coming to the end of the year. It is nearly Christmas time. And do you know the story of Christmas, and how it came about? We celebrate the birth of a child born thousands of years ago. Jesus Christ. Christians believe He was God, and this country was founded by Christians who believe this. But you need to know that not all religions believe this. So they may not celebrate Christmas, and that's ok too.

At your schools, I am sure you have children who have Jewish beliefs, or Muslim beliefs or Seventh Day Adventist beliefs, or who have no beliefs at all. We are all different. What we do when we are all different is learn about each other's faith and beliefs so we know what is important to them.

Poppy G and I went to a country where we were told by a taxi driver that the country had people who believed in about ten different religions. And he said, the people all celebrate them all. He laughed when he said that – this way they had more holidays and feasts, and happy days. Now that had to be one very clever country. Don't you just love that idea? The best of every religion is shared with everyone. The Holy Days, the Days of reverence, and no one takes offence, they just celebrate the lot. And what we noticed in their country was that everyone lived very peacefully. We thought it was magic.

Letter 31: December

Animals. I woke up today and thought about animals. I had seen a video of a baby elephant that was cared for by a dog, a large Alsatian. The strangest companions, but the Alsatian dog knew the baby elephant was not well so he stayed with him constantly. How did a dog know he was not well?

Dogs have something extra special about them - they seem to sense when everything is not happening as it should, and they care so much. I know one time when I was unwell, Toby, the golden retriever stayed so close to me I almost fell over him, many times. But he stayed, and snuggled up, and you would swear he knew and was trying to make me well again. They can be such a comfort, and they just seem to love without expecting anything in return. I wish we were all as noble as that.

That's your word for this letter. **Noble**

This word is described as showing excellence or superior quality. Or it could be someone of a higher rank. Doesn't Noble sound Noble! This is a word that sounds like the thing it is describing, and you understand all about that, don't you.

Are you beginning to get to see the magic of words, how they paint a picture, create a scene, make you feel someone's feelings? How magnificent is that. A single word can do that! So that means, you have to choose your words with care. We all have to.

Letter 32: December

I'm looking for an inspirational word. And then I thought of course 'inspiration' itself is a word – I have mentioned it before but it is such a lovely word to say and means such a lot. To inspire someone is to help them to be their creative self. Sometimes someone comes into our lives and we look up to them because they show us a way to behave. Their way is something that we like. Sometimes it might be a sporting person. But it could also be a person who we know who shows kindness to others, and they inspire us to be like them. Who do you know who is an inspiration for you? Who do you know that makes you think, 'Gee I would like to be just like them?'

Well, we can't always be just like them but we can learn to be very similar to them. For example, we can aspire to be like the great soccer players, so we try to play really well, as they do. Or we can aspire to be like a great Chef, and we can learn to cook really well, because someone inspires us.

So, you might just start to think one night when you are lying in bed, who would I 'like' to be like. A rally car driver? No, that's not me. A scientist, perhaps? I could be like one of the men and women who have travelled in space. Or a famous mathematician? Could I be like that? Or could I be like one of the designers of beautiful clothes? Well, you can be like any of these people – you just have to decide which one.

Letter 33: December

One day I hope you will be able to travel. When you travel, I would love for you to go to lots of other countries and to see how other people live. Why do I say that? Well, we live in Australia where most of us have homes and cars, and we have roads, and bridges, and towns and schools and hospitals. But that isn't the case for all countries.

So finding out how other people live is really important. And seeing some of the very old treasured buildings and the fine paintings, even seeing how others grow their vegetables is exciting, and different. I think when you live in one country you understand everything that is around you, but when you travel you begin to understand how the world actually is.

And there is another thing you find when you travel, you see different beautiful **landscapes**. *Hills, mountains, snow, rivers, flowers, and all of that can be quite magic. Now isn't that a lovely word, landscapes. That's when you are looking at the land all around you. And you really see the trees, and the fields. For some people when they see these beautiful landscapes, they want to paint the picture that they see.*

And maybe one day when you travel you will think of Nana, and look at the landscapes, and remember she said you would love them.

One thing I must warn you about. When you travel in other

countries, those people want to know about your country. So you had better be really well informed about your home country before you travel. They want to know if your country plays football, or soccer, if you have a Prime Minister, or a King. All sorts of things! How big is Australia? Do you have Kangaroos all over the country? What kind of houses do you live in? You see, they are just as interested in you, as you are in them. So it is lovely to share your knowledge of your own country with them. You could even take picture books with you if you were planning on going into countries that do not have schools like yours.

Letter 34: December

Festivities. That's your word for today. It is a word that has a happy ring to it. And it means having activities that are full of fun. Christmas time is a time of festivities and fun. But COVID has made this Christmas different. So to make it fun we have all had to do something to bring happy times to each other. I have a lady friend that I visit in hospital. Thinking how to bring her happy times in hospital can be quite hard work.

Now, if you were bringing me something to make me happy in hospital, it might be a 'talking book'. I love listening to someone reading. And Poppy G and I often play a 'Talking Book' while we are in the car on our long trips. We get to our destination, and we often just sit in the car while the reader finishes the chapter. Many really good books have been made into 'Talking Books' for those who cannot read anymore. Blind people enjoy them too.

Now, how would you get on being a reader and actually making a 'Talking Book?' I think that would be a lot of fun to do. I haven't seen any 'Talking Books' for children. I wonder if they are actually made for children too?

We are in the New Year!!

Letter 35: January 2021

We have begun a new year, and guess what? We will be leaving the COVID year behind us.

I am full of hope for 2021. I believe that people have the option of finding good in their world. Sometimes it may not seem that way. I guess sometimes it might seem like a sad old world, and while that may be true, it is up to you and to me to change our thoughts. We have to change them to happy thoughts.

How do you make happy thoughts? Well, I'll let you into a secret. The very first way you make these thoughts is by doing something different. You do something nice for yourself. And you have to remember Nana's special secret. You have to look up, because when you look up, you actually see things differently. Let's say it is sunny; you look up and see the blue sky, and the little clouds. And then you can say, wow I am warm under this sun, and how beautiful the sky colour is. And you start to feel a little better. Even if you look up and it is raining, you see the rain, and how it waters the garden, and you know it cleans the footpaths, fills up the tanks, and the dams. And you start to feel a little better.

Human beings are amazing people, don't you think? They have all these amazing ways of making themselves feel better, even when life is not being kind to us. So, you tuck this thought into your Grab bag of smart ideas. Nana said, "Look up." Gee whiz, Nana, how did you get to be so smart.

So Nana is going to let you into another secret of hers. She has listened to so many wise people who have told her so many wise stories that she now has her own Grab bag of ideas that she has collected along the way. And now she is telling them to you.

Letter 36 January

So school is going to restart for you both as January becomes February.

And is that exciting? Well, I hope so. What word would suit January and you going back to school?

Which one would you choose between trepidation and exhilaration?

Trepidation is when you are fearful of what is about to happen. **Exhilaration** is being super-excited. I wonder if you are a mixture of both, kind of frightened and excited too. I wonder what you would write in an essay if you had the Topic of "My First Day of School for 2021". If you wrote what you thought, and then kept a copy of this so that you could read it again in, say ten years' time, you might get the surprise of your life to see your thoughts.

I have a new word. It was a new word for me too. Someone called me an **epistlelorian**. It simply means someone who writes letters. But isn't it a grand title? I am going to tell everyone about this word; it has such a lovely sound to it. And that's me they are talking about, an epistlelorian. You can write that on my grave, Nana, the epistlelorian.

Letter 37: January

January is the time of new beginnings. And right now your new beginnings are a new school, or a new class. I am hoping that you both will go into this 'newness' with an excited heart. Looking at the new girls, or the new boys in your class, and making them feel warm and accepted. Talking with some of the 'new' faces and getting to know the person.

One thing I am sure of is that all new people to the class or the school all feel quite nervous, just like you. If you remember this then you will know what to say to them. And you will know how pleased they will be that you spoke to them. I remember in my first year at Secondary school, no one spoke to me. I didn't know which room was my classroom, or who my teachers were. That was really scary. So I told myself that the next year when all the new students came I would go around and speak to them and make them feel comfortable.

School is a pretty good place. I think you will both laugh at me for saying that. But it is a place where you can learn so much, and learning is exciting. I think it opens doors to other worlds. And that I find fascinating.

Imagine if you had an alien in your class. You would want to learn all about them and their country, just as they would want to learn all about you and your country.

What questions would you ask an Alien? Do you live in a house? What do aliens eat? Do you have any brothers, or *sisters? Can you kick a football?*

Now if I could give you an assignment it would be: How do you talk to an Alien from Outer Space! Let your imagination soar! What in the world would you ask them? Of course, I am assuming they can speak English. And if they couldn't how would you communicate with them? What a funny crazy world it would be trying to have a conversation with an Alien.

Letter 38: February

I wonder what you will think as you read the book that Nana wrote for you two.

Will you think, "WOW! A book written especially for us?" Or will you think, "Well, excuse me, but I have the MOST unusual Nana on the Planet."

Actually, I hope you think both those thoughts. Hey, you two, you may be immortalised by the book, and I sure don't mind being thought of as unusual.

My Nana was a kind lady, a very elegant lady, but also very strict. But my Poppa was a very, very gentle man, so all my memories of him are of such a lovely person. And it is funny the things you remember about people, isn't it? The most ridiculous things stick in your mind. Like my Aunty who made Hedgehogs for us to eat. Hedgehogs in New Zealand were little creatures that ran along on four legs and had long noses and very long spiky quills on their backs. My Aunt didn't make

real Hedgehogs, of course, but meat balls with rice that stuck out like prickles. She always said she would teach me how to make them, but unfortunately she never did.

Now you know that your Nana came from New Zealand to live in Australia. She came with your grandfather in 1975. She travelled over in a ship. It was a Russian Cruise ship and it was a very exciting experience. The food on board was decidedly strange and the hairdressing shop on board was even stranger. People sat under monstrous hair driers with enormous rollers in their hair – just like women did years and years ago. But the most unusual thing was – wait for this – the toilet paper. It was thick and grey and very hard. You couldn't even bend it, it was so tough. So isn't it strange what you remember.

Your two aunties and your uncle and your dad ran all over the ship and had a marvellous time. But when the clock said meal times, they were the first to line up at the dining room door, which was most embarrassing. They loved being able to choose what they had to eat each mealtime, and we always had to dress up for dinner because that was expected of us all. It was lots of fun.

And if you asked us would we do it all again? Of course! Coming to Australia changed our lives, but it was simply a change in our pathways of living. And some day you both will have different pathways to follow just like we did.

Letter 39: February

A word, a word, I am thinking of a word for this letter. ==Generous:== good, kind, selfless. A generous person gives because someone needs, not because they will be paid for what they give. Sometimes there are those who give generously even when they have very little to give. That's the person who shares their sandwich when they only really have enough for one person.

When Poppy G and Nana were in America on the 4th of July we went to the Boston Pops Orchestra completely by accident. We heard the music from our hotel and walked to find the Concert. The concert was in a huge Amphitheatre and we sat on the grass. Around us were people having picnics and lots of fun, and those around us insisted we join them and share their drinks, and their meal. We ended up having a wonderful night because people were so generous to us. They wanted to share their America with us and in return expected nothing. I remember Poppy and I left the Concert thinking that we had met some of the nicest people in the whole wide world.

Letter 40: March

This will be my last letter for this book.

I have loved writing to you and for you.

I have enjoyed talking to you both and I want you to know that the time I have spent writing for you has been very precious.

COVID may have made us stay at home. It may have made us all think about our friends and family, and about people in general, and this is perhaps the 'other side' of the misfortune of a Pandemic.

It actually gave us time to *pause.* And that is your last word for this book. To pause is just to slow down a little and to see the world with different eyes.

So the last thought I want to share with you is that it is absolutely perfectly ok to take a pause. When you and I look back at these months of COVID 19, you might remember that it has made us pause, and it gave us the chance to live in the present and to enjoy, and to laugh, and to care about one another.

Perhaps like me you can learn to develop a 'pause' button. And just enjoy the fact that you are loved, today, right now. And isn't that a cosy, teddy bear thought.

With deepest love,

Your Nana.

www.ingramcontent.com/pod-product-compliance
Lightning Source LLC
Chambersburg PA
CBHW051247110526
44588CB00025B/2913